BASKETBALL
ALL★STARS

By Alan Paul and Jon Kramer

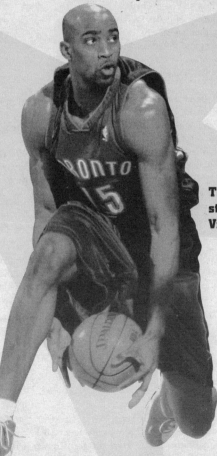

Toronto Raptor standout Vince Carter

A Sports Illustrated For Kids Book

Basketball All-Stars by Alan Paul and Jon Kramer

SPORTS ILLUSTRATED FOR KIDS and [Sports Illustrated KiDS] are registered trademarks of Time Inc.

Cover design by Emily Peterson Perez
Cover photographs by John W. McDonough/Sports Illustrated (Shaquille O'Neal) and Andy Hayt/NBA Photos (Vince Carter)
Interior photographs courtesy of NBA Photos
Interior design by Emily Peterson Perez
Research by Brian Holmes and Kathleen Fieffe

Basketball All-Stars is published by SPORTS ILLUSTRATED FOR KIDS, a division of Time Inc. Its trademark is registered in the U.S. Patent and Trademark Office and in other countries. SPORTS ILLUSTRATED FOR KIDS, 135 West 50th St., 4th Floor, New York, NY 10020-1393

For information, address: SPORTS ILLUSTRATED FOR KIDS

ISBN 1-930623-08-9

Printed in the United States of America

10 9 8 7 6 5 4 3 2 1

Basketball All-Stars is a production of SPORTS ILLUSTRATED FOR KIDS Books:
Cathrine Wolf, Assistant Managing Editor; Emily Peterson Perez, Art Director;
Margaret Sieck, Senior Editor; Aaron Derr and Jon Kramer (Project Editor),
Associate Editors; Robert J. Rohr, Copy Manager;
Erin Tricarico, Photo Researcher; Ron Beuzenburg, Production Manager

Contents

Introduction

The NBA is driven by stars whom most fans have heard about for years. We all have our favorites. Some are great dunkers while others are known for their passing or shooting skills. Big guys, small guys: The NBA is a pretty diverse group. People pick their favorite players for all kinds of reasons.

Basketball All-Stars is your guide to the 22 best players in the sport. We selected a five-player starting lineup for both the Eastern and Western Conferences. These are the best players at each position. There are big-name veterans like center Shaquille O'Neal and forward Grant Hill. There are young superstars like guards Allen Iverson and Kobe Bryant. And don't forget fan favorites such as forwards Vince Carter, Tim Duncan, and Kevin Garnett.

It was tough to select just 10 All-Stars, so we also chose some honorable mentions. These are the players who didn't quite make our starting lineup. This section includes John Stockton, the NBA's all-time assist leader, and Karl Malone, perhaps the greatest power forward in league history. The book also includes "Stars of the Future," like Elton Brand and Steve Francis. And we didn't want to forget Charles Barkley, so we honored him in our "Tribute" section.

We think you'll find the NBA's most exciting players in this book. So turn the pages to get the scoop! Find out why these 22 men deserve to be called *Basketball All-Stars*. ★

Eastern Conference Starting Lineup

F	**Vince Carter, Toronto Raptors**
F	**Grant Hill, Orlando Magic**
C	**Alonzo Mourning, Miami Heat**
G	**Allen Iverson, Philadelphia 76ers**
G	**Reggie Miller, Indiana Pacers**

VINCE CARTER

Forward/Guard, Toronto Raptors
Born: January 26, 1977, in Daytona Beach, Florida
Height: 6' 6"
Weight: 225 pounds
Entered NBA: 1998

Vince Carter was already a fast-rising NBA star with a growing number of devoted fans. Then, on February 11, 2000, that changed. That night, the acrobatic guard of the Toronto Raptors became the hottest basketball star on the planet!

It happened at the NBA slam-dunk contest, in Oakland, California. Vince didn't just win the electrifying event of high-flying moves. He blew away the competition! He

Nicknamed Air Canada, Vince has a 41-inch vertical leap.

thrilled fans and his fellow All-Stars with an unbelievable display of rim-rattling dunks.

Vince's moves are so cool they can turn anyone into a smiling kid — including other NBA players. Shaquille O'Neal of the Los Angeles Lakers calls Vince his favorite player. At the slam-dunk contest, Shaquille sat on the floor video-taping Vince like an awestruck fan. Allen Iverson of the Philadelphia 76ers ran off the court afterward, screaming "Vin-sanity, baby, I love it!"

FAST FACTS

☆Was a finalist for the 1999 NBA Sportsmanship Award

☆Has played saxophone since he was 10 years old

☆Left college after his junior year, but earned his degree in African-American studies during the summer of 2000

Smashing slam dunks are fine, but Vince wants to be known for more. "Dunkers come and go," he says. "You can go down to the playground and find a bunch of guys who can do fancy dunks. The great players excel at all aspects of the game. That's what I want to do."

Vince made a spectacular start toward that goal. He won the NBA's Rookie of the Year award in 1998-99, when he averaged 18.3 points per game. In 1999-2000, his scoring average jumped to 25.7 points per game. Vince also improved in rebounding, shooting percentage, 3-point shooting, assists, and steals.

"The first time I played against him, I said, 'If this kid gets a jump shot, he's going to be awesome,' " says Dan Majerle of the Miami Heat. "He developed one pretty quick. If he continues to work on his game and not be satisfied, the sky's the limit."

Even Vince is amazed how fast his star has risen. "I just pinch myself and say, 'Wow, is it really happening?' " he says. "It's great, though."

Vince is often compared to Michael Jordan. Vince has an amazing 41-inch vertical leap. That means he can jump nearly three-and-a-half feet off the ground! Michael had a great vertical leap, too, and could fly through the air making amazing moves, just like Vince does. In addition, both Vince and Michael went to the University of North Carolina and left after their junior seasons.

> **"If he continues to work on his game and not be satisfied, the sky's the limit."**
> **— Dan Majerle, Miami Heat guard**

Many people think Michael is the greatest athlete of all time. "It's a great compliment [to be compared to Michael]," Vince says. "But I'm more interested in establishing my own identity. I just play. I just continue to do the things that I know I can do."

Actually, Vince looks to improve on the things he already does well while learning new skills to make him even better. He isn't satisfied with what he has accomplished. And he tries not to talk about his unique talents.

"I try to stay away from things like how high I can jump," Vince says. "I just work on persistence and perfection. I want to go for perfection."

For opponents, that is perfectly frightening!   ★

GRANT HILL

Forward, Orlando Magic
Born: October 5, 1972, in Dallas, Texas
Height: 6' 8"
Weight: 225 pounds
Entered NBA: 1994

Looking for a role model? Most kids are. Many choose professional athletes. Others choose their parents Grant Hill of the Orlando Magic chose both — without even trying.

Grant looked up to his parents, teachers, and coaches. It just so happened that his father, Calvin, was a pro athlete. Mr. Hill was a fine running back with the NFL's Dallas Cowboys, Washington Redskins, and Cleveland Browns.

Grant has worked hard recently to improve his outside shot.

Growing up as the son of a pro athlete was a mixed blessing, according to Grant. "I was always expected to be the best athlete because of my father. It didn't matter if I was playing kick the can," he says. "But I also got to go with my dad to football and basketball games and meet a lot of people. I thought that was fun."

Grant remains extremely close to his dad and to his mother, Janet. He usually speaks to one of them every day. "They're a big part of my life and success," he says.

And Grant has had plenty of success! He is one of the best — and best-known — players in the NBA. After six seasons with the Detroit Pistons, Grant signed with the Magic during the summer of 2000. His contract was worth $67.5 million over six years!

Grant burst on the basketball scene when he was a student at Duke University, in Durham, North Carolina. He helped the Blue Devils win back-to-back NCAA championships during the 1990-91 and 1991-92 seasons. In 1994, he entered the NBA. Grant shared the Rookie of the Year award with Jason Kidd and led the Pistons in scoring. He also became the first rookie in NBA history to lead the league in fan voting for the All-Star Game!

FAST FACTS

☆ Was vice-chairman of the 1999 Special Olympic World Games, which were held in North Carolina
☆ Had his uniform number (33) retired at Duke University
☆ Lists his sports idols as former tennis star Arthur Ashe and basketball great Julius Erving

The next season, Grant led Detroit in points, rebounds, and assists. Grant has been a triple threat ever since. If he had any weakness in his first few pro seasons, it was his jump shot. But Grant worked with a shooting coach during the summer of 1999 to improve his shot. It worked! During the 1999-2000 season, Grant knocked down jumpers left and right. He attempted more 3-pointers than ever before. He scored an average of 25.8 points per game, a career best and the third-highest average in the league.

> "Grant is a Michael Jordan-type player."
> — Don Chaney, New York Knick assistant coach

"Grant is a Michael Jordan-type player," says Don Chaney, an assistant coach with the New York Knicks. "He is a great one-on-one player, a great penetrator, and a great passer off the dribble. He puts up great all-around numbers every night, and does the little things that help his team win."

What Grant really wants is to win the big prize: the NBA Championship. He got used to that winning feeling at Duke.

But Grant learned a whole lot more than basketball in college. "I learned how to use my time wisely," he says. "Juggling schoolwork, basketball, and a social life is tough. I had to learn to do that if I wanted to be a success."

Apparently, he learned his lessons well. Grant has become a major success — and a pretty good role model, too. ★

ALONZO MOURNING

Center, Miami Heat
Born: February 8, 1970, in Chesapeake, Virginia
Height: 6' 10"
Weight: 261 pounds
Entered NBA: 1992

The first thing you notice is the scowl. Alonzo Mourning of the Miami Heat is very intense on the basketball court — and his face reflects that intensity. Looking for a smile? Better wait until after the game.

"I love him," says former NBA star Charles Barkley. "He's a serious warrior. He goes after every shot, and he works really hard. That's all you can ask of a player."

Alonzo has always been intense. During a 1998 playoff game, he got into a fight with Larry Johnson of the New York Knicks. That inspired Knick coach Jeff Van Gundy to run onto the court. Coach Van Gundy latched onto Alonzo's leg like a pit bull. He held on for dear life as Alonzo dragged him across the floor!

"My intensity is part of my game," says Alonzo. "It gets me up and ready to play."

When the game ends, though, it's a different story. Alonzo becomes a real sweetheart. In 1997, he founded "Zo's Summer Groove." It's a big event that is held every year in Miami to raise money for two groups; the Children's Home Society and 100 Black Men of South Florida. The Groove consists of a banquet, concert, and celebrity basketball game.

Alonzo does a lot of charity work, with most of it geared toward children. But he's good to adults, too. Several years ago, a Florida man lost everything he owned in a fire. Alonzo gave him shirts, shoes, and suits — right out of his own closet. That was generous!

On the basketball court, however, Alonzo doesn't give anything away. During the 1999-2000 season, he led the league in blocked shots, with an average of 3.7 per

What a competitor! Alonzo is intense once the game starts.

FAST FACTS

☆In 1999, finished second in NBA MVP voting behind Karl Malone of the Utah Jazz

☆One of his best friends is Patrick Ewing of the New York Knicks

☆Earned a degree in sociology from Georgetown University

game. Alonzo was named the NBA's Defensive Player of the Year for the second consecutive season. But he's not just the league's best defender, he's also the league's *most feared* defender. No one wants to challenge him under the basket!

Alonzo had a great career at Georgetown University, in Washington, D.C., before entering the NBA, in 1992, with the Charlotte Hornets. He was traded to the Heat three years later. Alonzo has helped Miami become a power in the Eastern Conference. And despite being one of the league's highest-paid players, he never stops working.

"I love him. He's a serious warrior . . . He goes after every shot, and he works really hard. That's all you can ask of a player."
— Charles Barkley, former NBA great

"He's there early, and he's the last one to leave," says former teammate Jamal Mashburn. "A lot of All-Stars *talk* about doing that, but he does it . . . Zo's special."

Alonzo had a terrific season in 1999-2000. In addition to all those blocks, he averaged 21.7 points and 9.5 rebounds per game. He shot an impressive 55 percent from the field. Alonzo used to score most of his points on slams, tip-ins, and short shots around the hoop. Over the past few years, he's developed a good outside shot.

"He can . . . put the ball on the floor and drive to the basket," says Don Chaney, an assistant coach with the rival New York Knicks. "Alonzo is also one of the best rebounders and shot blockers in the league."

And one of the most caring, too — despite the scowl! ★

ALLEN IVERSON

Guard, Philadelphia 76ers
Born: **June 7, 1975, in Hampton, Virginia**
Height: **6'**
Weight: **165 pounds**
Entered NBA: **1996**

Allen Iverson has led the NBA in scoring. He's one of the league's most exciting players. He led the Philadelphia 76ers to the playoffs two seasons in a row, after a seven-year absence. So why do so many people, including his own coach, criticize the flashy guard?

Some people don't like his tattoos and brash attitude. Others say he shoots too much and doesn't play defense. Sixers coach Larry

Allen is a great player, but a contoversial one, too.

15

Brown has questioned Allen's commitment to the team. But Allen has learned to shrug off such complaints.

"There are going to be guys out there who are constantly criticizing me, especially now that I have led the league in scoring," Allen says. "I know that. I think there are going to be a billion people out there who respect my game and a billion people who dislike it. I understand that, so that's what keeps me moving forward."

Allen has never had a problem filling the hoop. He was named the NBA's Rookie of the Year in 1996-97, after averaging 23.5 points per game. In one game that season, on April 12, 1997, he exploded for 50 points against the Cleveland Cavaliers! Two years later, in 1998-99, he averaged 26.8 points per game to lead the league. Then he improved that number to 28.4 in 1999-2000. Only MVP Shaquille O'Neal of the Los Angeles Lakers had a better average (29.7).

> "I love Iverson's courage. He's not afraid to take a hit."
> — Jeff Van Gundy, New York Knick coach

"Allen is a great scorer with unbelievable quickness, and he can get to the basket at will," says New York Knick assistant coach Don Chaney.

Although he's just 6' and 165 pounds, Allen isn't shy about driving to the hoop. He shows no fear, often battling opponents a foot taller who weigh nearly twice as much. Allen is remarkably tough, and he has kept playing despite several injuries.

"I love Iverson's courage," says Knick coach Jeff Van Gundy. "He's not afraid to take a hit."

Coach Van Gundy sounds as if he were talking about a football player. That's appropriate because Allen played football, in addition to basketball, at Bethel High School, in Hampton, Virginia. He was an outstanding quarterback and was named the state's Player of the Year as a junior!

FAST FACTS

☆ Named First Team All-NBA in 1998-99 after leading the league in scoring

☆ Made history in 1996-97 by becoming the first Sixer to win the league's Rookie of the Year award

☆ Had five consecutive games with 40 or more points as a rookie

Allen could have played football in college, but he chose to concentrate on basketball, at Georgetown University, in Washington, D.C. After two outstanding seasons, Allen left school and became the first player selected in the 1996 NBA draft.

Even though Allen has enjoyed much success, he knows there's room for more. "I have been learning every aspect of the game," he says. "I know it takes time and I have a long way to go, but . . . [I'm] learning how to play the game a little bit more."

That's bad news for Allen's opponents. Now try telling it to his critics! ★

REGGIE MILLER

Guard, Indiana Pacers
Born: August 24, 1965, in Riverside, California
Height: 6' 7"
Weight: 185 pounds
Entered NBA: 1987

There's a minute left in the game. The score is tied and tension fills the arena. Who wants the ball in that situation? Reggie Miller, that's who. The sweet-shooting guard of the Indiana Pacers wants the game in *his* hands.

"I've always considered myself a crunch-time player," says Reggie. "The more eyes that are on you, the more intense you become. You can't be scared to fail. You can't make every game-winning shot, but you can believe that you can."

Reggie thrives under pressure. His late-game heroics have helped Indiana become a power in the NBA's Eastern Conference. They also earned him spots on the 1994 U.S. national team and the 1996 U.S. Olympic team. Reggie's greatest strength is his ability to get open, even in those tense situations when everyone is watching him.

Reggie is also one of the game's best foul shooters. He has made 88.1 percent of them in his career. That's the seventh-highest figure in NBA history and the best among active players! How did he become such a good shooter? Reggie says it's simple. "Practice makes perfect. Repetition. There's no getting around that."

FAST FACTS

☆ Enjoys making surprise visits to schools around central Indiana
☆ Started a foundation to assist fire victims after losing his own house in a fire on May 15, 1997
☆ Played college ball at UCLA, finishing third on the Bruins' all-time scoring list with 2,095 points

Many NBA stars don't like playing on the road. Reggie isn't one of them. He enjoys it, especially when he plays in places like Madison Square Garden, the home of the New York Knicks. In a 1995 playoff game at the Garden, he scored 8 points in 8.9 seconds to give the Pacers a big win. The New York fans have never forgiven him. They shower him with boos! But it doesn't bother Reggie. It makes him even more determined to succeed.

Reggie is one of the greatest shooters in NBA history.

19

"There's got to be people that everyone loves to hate," he says. "I just happen to be [one of those people]. I like wearing the black hat."

Reggie has worn the *Pacers'* hat during his entire 13-year career. He led the team in scoring every season from 1989-99. Reggie has averaged 19.5 points per game during his career. In the pressure-filled playoffs, though, his average is 23.2! He's also the NBA's all-time leader in 3-point baskets with 1,867.

> **"You can't be scared to fail. You can't make every game-winning shot, but you can believe that you can."**
> **— Reggie Miller, Indiana Pacer guard**

Reggie grew up in Riverside, California. As a boy, he wasn't even the best basketball player in his family. His sister Cheryl was! Cheryl grew up to be one of the best players in the women's game. She led the University of Southern California to two NCAA championships in the 1980's and is now the head coach/general manager of the WNBA's Phoenix Mercury. Other playmates included brother Darrell, who later played major league baseball with the California Angels, and sister Tammy, who played volleyball in college.

"I got involved in playing ball just by hanging around my older brothers and sisters," Reggie says. "They all played, so I got into it."

Reggie has already gotten into broadcasting, too. During the summer, he works on WNBA telecasts. When the game is on the line, he wants the microphone. Would you expect anything else?　　★

Western Conference Starting Lineup

F	Kevin Garnett, Minnesota Timberwolves
F	Tim Duncan, San Antonio Spurs
C	Shaquille O'Neal, Los Angeles Lakers
G	Kobe Bryant, Los Angeles Lakers
G	Gary Payton, Seattle SuperSonics

KEVIN GARNETT

Forward, Minnesota Timberwolves
Born: May 19, 1976, in Mauldin, South Carolina
Height: 6' 11"
Weight: 220 pounds
Entered NBA: 1995

In 1995, Kevin Garnett made the biggest decision of his life. He decided to become a professional basketball player even though he had just graduated from Ferragut Academy, in Chicago, Illinois. A lot of people thought Kevin was crazy! At the time, only four U.S. players had jumped directly from high school to the NBA. Only one — Moses Malone — had become a big star.

Kevin wasn't worried. He believed he had the talent and maturity to play in the NBA. So did the Minnesota Timberwolves, who selected him fifth overall in the 1995 NBA draft.

They were *all* right. Kevin became a solid player immediately and improved his point, rebound, and assist totals in each of his first five seasons. In 1999-2000, he averaged 22.9 points, 11.8 rebounds, and 5 assists per game. He also continued to improve defensively. Despite being almost seven feet tall, Kevin is quick and agile. He can shoot, pass, and dribble like a guard. He can also dominate a game under the boards.

"Each time you see [Kevin] play, you see him improve," says Frank Hamblen, an assistant coach with the Los Angeles Lakers. "He is a great athlete who can run the floor, score on the break, handle the ball, shoot jump shots, play defense — he can do it all."

Since Kevin jumped to the pros, an increasing number of high school players have followed suit. Kevin hopes they're not doing so because of his success. He says each individual must make his own judgment.

"I've always said that my decision was a decision that Kevin Maurice Garnett had to

Kevin's engaging personality has made him a fan favorite.

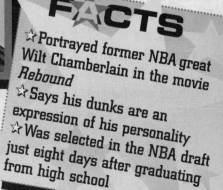

FAST FACTS

☆ Portrayed former NBA great Wilt Chamberlain in the movie *Rebound*

☆ Says his dunks are an expression of his personality

☆ Was selected in the NBA draft just eight days after graduating from high school

make for himself," he says. "I felt this was the best thing and I did it."

Kevin's decision worked for him. He quickly became one of the NBA's best players. He's one of its most popular, too, thanks to his colorful play and upbeat personality. That personality showed in a funny television commercial he did for Nike with soccer star Brandi Chastain.

Kevin lives in suburban Minneapolis with a group of his old friends from Mauldin, South Carolina. (Kevin lived in Mauldin until his senior year of high school.) The group even has a name, the Official Block Family, or OBF. They are starting a clothing line with the same title. Kevin is good to his friends.

"My idea is, 'I shine, you shine,' " Kevin says. "If I'm doing well and you're with me, you do well."

**"He is a great athlete who can run the floor, score on the break, handle the ball, shoot jump shots, play defense — he can do it all."
— Frank Hamblen, Los Angeles Laker assistant coach**

And as long as Kevin is playing hoops, he feels well.

"Basketball gives me a sense of relief," Kevin says. "No matter what kind of disturbance I have in life, I can always go to the court and just release it.

"That's what I love about basketball. It's like a book. With a book you can just disappear because you are so into what you're reading. So basketball is my book."

In Kevin's case, that book is turning out to be a best-seller! ★

TIM DUNCAN

Forward, San Antonio Spurs
Born: April 25, 1976, in St. Croix, Virgin Islands
Height: 7'
Weight: 260 pounds
Entered NBA: 1997

Tim Duncan grew up on the island of St. Croix, in the Caribbean Sea. He's an excellent swimmer, but there's one thing in the blue ocean water that has always frightened him: sharks!

Sharks may be the only thing in the world that upsets the San Antonio Spur forward. He's certainly not afraid of anything on the basketball court.

Tim became one of the NBA's best players almost

Why is Tim so good? That's easy. Simply put, he does *everything* well.

25

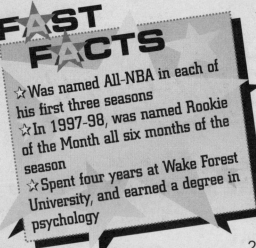

FAST FACTS

☆ Was named All-NBA in each of his first three seasons

☆ In 1997-98, was named Rookie of the Month all six months of the season

☆ Spent four years at Wake Forest University, and earned a degree in psychology

the moment he entered the league, in 1997. He played in the All-Star Game and won the Rookie of the Year award. He also became just the ninth rookie in league history to make the All-NBA team. Tim averaged 21.1 points and 11.9 rebounds per game. Coach Jerry Sloan of the Utah Jazz called him the best rookie he had ever seen.

The bad news for opponents is that Tim just keeps getting better. When Michael Jordan retired after the 1997-98 season, Tim was quickly hailed as the league's best all-around player. The pressure to live up to that kind of hype would derail many players. Not Tim! Getting nervous or getting a swelled head has never been a problem for him.

"I go out there and . . . try to do the best I can," he explains. "I don't worry about what people want me to do or expect me to do."

Adds Gregg Popovich, the Spurs' general manager and coach: "I haven't seen anything faze Tim Duncan. Whether he does something well or poorly, he goes on to the next task at hand. He just isn't bothered by any of it. It doesn't matter how he plays. He is going to continue to try and do his best, and usually that's what he does."

Tim led the Spurs to their first NBA championship, in 1998-99, and was named MVP of the Finals. It was just his second NBA season! "This is the best feeling in the world," he said after receiving the MVP award. "You can't ask for much more."

The following season, Tim ranked among the Top 10 in the league in points, rebounds, blocked shots, and minutes played. He averaged 23.2 points, 12.4 rebounds, 2.23 blocked shots, and 38.9 minutes per game. He can do just about anything on the court.

"There's not a man on the planet who can stop Duncan," says coach Jeff Van Gundy of the New York Knicks. "He's going to get big numbers."

Tim spent four years in college. He had time to mature as a player and a person before turning pro. He capped his great career at Wake Forest University, in Winston-Salem, North Carolina, by winning several Player of the Year awards as a senior. Then he jumped right into NBA stardom.

> **"His progress is overwhelming. He's clearly a dominant player, and it is really something that he has done it so quickly."**
> **— Allan Houston, New York Knick guard**

"His progress is overwhelming," said Knick guard Allan Houston. "He's clearly a dominant player, and it is really something that he has done it so quickly." ★

SHAQUILLE O'NEAL

Center, Los Angeles Lakers
Born: March 6, 1972, in Newark, New Jersey
Height: 7' 1"
Weight: 315 pounds
Entered NBA: 1992

As a rookie, in 1992-93, Shaquille O'Neal led the NBA in turnovers. Eight seasons later, he led the NBA in a few other things, such as scoring, field-goal percentage, and MVP awards. The overpowering center also led his Los Angeles Lakers to the NBA Championship, finally fulfilling the huge expectations that had hovered over him since that rookie year.

Shaq could always score, but it took him awhile to become a truly outstanding player. In 1999-2000, he led the NBA in points per game, with 29.7. He finished second in rebounds (13.6), third in blocked shots (3.03), and fourth in minutes played (40). Why Shaq even led NBA centers in assists, with 299 in 79 games! About the only thing he didn't do well consistently was shoot free throws (52.4 percent). He is working on that.

"Shaq is a monster around the basket at both ends of the court," says Frank Hamblen, an assistant coach with the Lakers.

Shaq dominated the voting for MVP of the 1999-2000 season. He earned 120 of 121 possible first-place votes! (Allen Iverson of the Philadelphia 76ers got the other.) Shaq shared the MVP award for the All-Star Game with Tim Duncan of the San Antonio Spurs, and was named MVP of the NBA Finals. In that series, Shaq was nearly unstoppable. He *averaged* 38 points, 16.7 rebounds, and 2.7 blocks per game. When Los Angeles defeated the Indiana Pacers to win the title, he cried during the celebration. That's how badly he wanted a championship.

Shaq's title was a long time coming. He has been a powerful force since beginning his NBA career with the Orlando Magic. In 1995, he helped the Magic reach the

FAST FACTS

☆His first and middle names, Shaquille Rashaun, mean "Little Warrior" in Islam

☆Has recorded five rap albums and appeared in several motion pictures, including *Blue Chips* and *Steel*

☆Played three years of college ball at Louisiana State University (LSU)

Off the court, Shaq is a gentle giant with a soft spot for children.

NBA Finals, but they were swept by the Houston Rockets. One year later, he signed with Los Angeles and helped revive a sagging Laker franchise. Along the way, he became a big-name personality, pursuing side careers in acting and rap music.

Shaq has always stood out from the crowd. In the NBA, he makes other centers look like munchkins. Imagine how big he looked next to other children.

"It was good and bad being so big as a kid," Shaq says. "I was picked first for kickball games. But some kids made fun of me, so I became sort of a bully. I felt I had to be mean, because then they knew not to mess with me."

Shaq is actually something of a gentle giant who enjoys doing good deeds, especially for children. He created "Shaqsgiving" and "Shaqschristmas" to help needy families in Los Angeles. On Shaqsgiving, he hands out turkey at a shelter. Then he dresses up as Shaq-a-Claus and distributes presents before Christmas. Shaq credits his mother and father with teaching him the importance of helping others. His parents also gave him the confidence to succeed.

> **"Shaq is a monster around the basket at both ends of the court."**
> **— Frank Hamblen, Los Angeles Laker assistant coach**

"They always told me that I could be whatever I wanted to be," Shaq says. "I've learned that if you are willing to dream, anything can be accomplished."

An NBA title, MVP awards, scoring championships, millions of dollars . . . this big man must have had some *big* dreams! ★

KOBE BRYANT

Guard, Los Angeles Lakers
Born: August 23, 1978, in Philadelphia, Pennsylvania
Height: 6' 7"
Weight: 210 pounds
Entered NBA: 1996

Kobe Bryant wasn't under any pressure to jump straight from high school to the NBA without playing college basketball. The Los Angeles Laker guard had the grades and test scores to go to college. He scored an impressive 1,080 on the SAT entrance exam.

Money wasn't a concern, either. Kobe's father, Joe "Jelly Bean" Bryant, played in the NBA and the Italian professional league. The

Kobe and Shaquille O'Neal form a great 1-2 punch for the Lakers.

family was very comfortable and didn't need Kobe to get a job at age 18.

No, Kobe didn't have to turn pro. He just wanted to. "Playing in the NBA has been my dream since I was three," he told *Sports Illustrated* in 1996, when he made his decision. Lucky for Kobe, he was good enough to make the jump.

Kobe lived in Italy from age 5 to 14 while his dad was playing pro basketball there. As a result, Kobe learned to play the sport in an unusual way. He watched NBA games on videotapes, sent by his grandparents, then practiced the moves he saw. Kobe copied everyone from center Hakeem Olajuwon of the Houston Rockets to his hero, point guard Magic Johnson of the Lakers.

"I was like a computer," Kobe says. "I retrieved information to benefit my game."

If he had lived in America, Kobe would have probably started playing organized basketball at an early age. In Italy, all his friends played soccer, so Kobe played basketball by himself or with his father and other pros. After school, Kobe went to work with his dad. While Mr. Bryant's team practiced, Kobe shot hoops at a corner basket. At halftime of games, he

FAST FACTS

☆His parents named him after a Kobe steak restaurant because they liked the way the name sounded
☆Speaks fluent Italian and is half owner of an Italian basketball team called Olimpia Milano
☆Has two older sisters, Sharia and Shaya

played on the court before being shooed away so the games could resume!

"The crowd would be cheering me," Kobe recalls. "I loved it."

The crowds still cheer Kobe. He became one of the NBA's most popular players as soon as he joined the Lakers, in 1996. Four years later, he and center Shaquille O'Neal, helped by new coach Phil Jackson, led the Lakers to their first NBA title in 12 years! Kobe played a key role in Game 4 of the NBA Finals, against the Indiana Pacers. When Shaq fouled out in overtime, Kobe took charge. He scored 8 points in the extra session to help the Lakers win a key contest.

Kobe has thrived in the spotlight, embracing his role as a star. Some players are bothered by the pressure. Kobe enjoys it. "It's a lot of fun," he

> "Playing in the NBA has been my dream since I was three."
> — Kobe Bryant, Los Angeles Laker guard

says. "We've all watched the NBA growing up. We've all seen Magic, [Larry] Bird, and Michael [Jordan], and to be talked about in the same breath is an honor. It's far from being a burden."

Clearly, Kobe made the right decision going pro when he did. He has a championship ring on his finger and played in two All-Star Games before turning 22! But few players can make that jump from high school to the NBA. Right now, there's probably a youngster studying Kobe's moves on videotape. What a player *that* kid is going to grow up to be! ★

GARY PAYTON

Guard, Seattle SuperSonics
Born: July 23, 1968, in Oakland, California
Height: 6' 4"
Weight: 180 pounds
Entered NBA: 1990

"The Glove" may seem like a strange nickname for a basketball player, but that's what people call Seattle SuperSonic star Gary Payton — and it's perfect!

Gary is the best defensive guard in the NBA. That's how he earned his nickname. When Seattle played the Phoenix Suns in the 1993 NBA Western Conference Finals, Gary guarded Kevin Johnson of the Suns. Gary covered Kevin so well that the all-star had trouble scoring.

A cousin called Gary during the series and said, "You're holding Kevin Johnson like a baseball in a glove." Gary has been known as "The Glove" ever since.

Gary has been named to the NBA's All-Defensive team seven seasons in a row. But as good as he is defensively, it's just a part of what makes him so valuable. He's also a dynamic scorer, a rugged rebounder, and a terrific passer.

Gary had trouble filling the hoop when he first entered the NBA. In college, it wasn't a problem: Gary averaged 25.7 points per game during his senior year at Oregon State University.

But Gary struggled against the tough NBA defenses. He averaged only 7.2 points per game during his rookie season and 9.4 in his second. Gary worked hard to become a top-notch shooter. He was scoring over 20 points per game by his fifth season. And in 1999-2000, he averaged 24.2 points per contest, the seventh-highest figure in the NBA.

"One reason he's so frustrating to play against is that he gets it done on both ends [of the court]," says Sonic guard Vernon Maxwell. "He scores on you, then he turns right around and starts playing

What a mouth! Gary might be the best trash talker in the NBA!

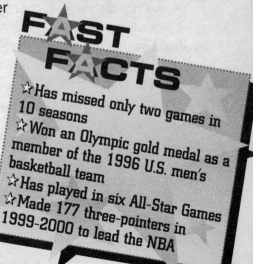

FAST FACTS

☆ Has missed only two games in 10 seasons

☆ Won an Olympic gold medal as a member of the 1996 U.S. men's basketball team

☆ Has played in six All-Star Games

☆ Made 177 three-pointers in 1999-2000 to lead the NBA

some of the best defense in the NBA."

Gary also frustrates opponents with his endless stream of trash talk. "You can't beat me" is probably one of the nicer things he tells them! Center Greg Foster, a current Sonic and former high school teammate of Gary's, says the guard has always been able to unnerve opponents. "For as long as I've known Gary, he's been getting the mental edge like that," says Greg.

Greg is one of several current NBA players who grew up in Oakland, California, playing with or against Gary on the playground. Others include Antonio Davis, a forward with the Toronto Raptors; J.R. Rider, a forward who spent the 1999-2000 season with the Atlanta Hawks; and Jason Kidd, the all-star guard of the Phoenix Suns.

> "He's an unbelievable competitor and one of the best players I've ever seen on both ends of the court."
> — Larry Brown, coach of the Philadelphia 76ers

Jason says that he learned much of what he knows about the game from Gary. "One time we were playing, and he wouldn't let me get a shot off at all," recalls Jason. "He was just trying to show me that it's going to take a lot more than just being stronger than the other guys."

For 10 seasons now, Gary has been giving similar lessons to NBA guards. He's made himself into a complete player.

"He's an unbelievable competitor and one of the best players I've ever seen on both ends of the court," says coach Larry Brown of the Philadelphia 76ers.

The description fits Gary like a glove!   ★

Honorable Mentions

With so many talented players in the NBA, selecting an All-Star lineup is a difficult task. It's impossible to choose just 10 players! That's why we created an "Honorable Mentions" chapter.

The seven players you will read about on the following pages are truly all-star caliber. Some, like John Stockton and Karl Malone of the Utah Jazz, are future Hall of Famers. The same can be said of Scottie Pippen, who played on six NBA championship teams with the Chicago Bulls, and David Robinson of the San Antonio Spurs. These men did not make our starting lineup, but still deserve to be called all-stars.

Our other honorable-mention picks are Jason Kidd of the Phoenix Suns, Chris Webber of the Sacramento Kings, and Stephon Marbury of the New Jersey Nets. They're all exciting players who can take over a game.

You might feel that some of our honorable mentions should be in the starting lineup, instead of the players we picked. That's fine with us. Part of the fun of sports is debating which players are best! ★

DAVID ROBINSON

Center, San Antonio Spurs
Born: August 6, 1965, in Key West, Florida
Height: 7' 1"
Weight: 250 pounds
Entered NBA: 1989

David Robinson is not an ordinary guy. He took college computer classes while still in junior high! He has a college degree in mathematics and he attained the rank of lieutenant junior grade in the U.S. Navy. He can play the piano and saxophone.

Since entering the NBA in 1989, David has put up some eye-popping numbers. The center of the San Antonio Spurs has averaged 23.7 points and 11.3 rebounds

David served in the Navy before beginning his NBA career.

per game in 11 seasons. Quick and agile, he's a good shooter with some nifty moves around the basket.

David has always believed in challenging himself. Growing up in Manassas, Virginia, near Washington, D.C., he thought he might become a scientist. He didn't play on an organized basketball team until his senior year of high school.

When it came time to choose a college, David was not thinking about an NBA career. He entered the U.S. Naval Academy, in Annapolis, Maryland, in 1983. Then he grew seven inches

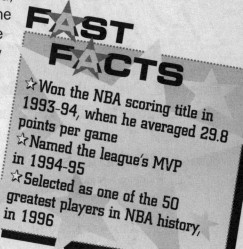

FAST FACTS

☆ Won the NBA scoring title in 1993-94, when he averaged 29.8 points per game
☆ Named the league's MVP in 1994-95
☆ Selected as one of the 50 greatest players in NBA history, in 1996

at the academy and became the best player in college basketball! The Spurs drafted him first overall in 1987, but had to wait two years while he served in the Navy.

David had some great seasons in San Antonio, but one thing was missing — an NBA title. He finally got it in 1999 after accepting a lesser role in the Spur offense. David was asked to concentrate on defense while Tim Duncan became the leading scorer. David did it for the good of the team.

"He is a rare superstar because he is not ruled by his ego, and for a coach, that's a treasure," says Gregg Popovich, the Spurs' head coach and general manager.

As we said, David is not an ordinary guy! ★

SCOTTIE PIPPEN

Forward, Portland Trail Blazers
Born: September 25, 1965, in Hamburg, Arkansas
Height: 6' 7"
Weight: 228 pounds
Entered NBA: 1987

Question: If forward Scottie Pippen has never led the NBA in scoring, rebounding, assists, or blocked shots, why was he chosen, in 1996, as one of the 50 greatest players in the league's history?

Answer: Because the Portland Trail Blazer standout does a little bit of everything very well. Scottie averaged 17.3 points, 6.7 rebounds, and 5.3 assists per game through his first 13 NBA seasons (1987-2000). But those great numbers only tell half the story! Scottie is also an outstanding defender. His long arms and awesome quickness allow him to cover opponents like a wet blanket.

"He may be the best defensive player ever," says forward Karl Malone of the Utah Jazz.

That's high praise for someone few people had heard of before the 1987 NBA draft. The Seattle SuperSonics chose

Scottie that year and immediately traded him to Chicago. The Bulls had Michael Jordan but little else. They needed another scoring threat to keep opposing teams from focusing entirely on Michael. Scottie became that threat, and the Bulls became a dynasty! They won six NBA championships between 1991 and 1998. Michael provided the sizzle while Scottie added extra punch, especially on defense.

After the Bulls won their sixth title, in 1998, Michael retired, and Scottie was traded to the Houston Rockets. One season later, on October 2, 1999, Scottie was traded to Portland. He helped the Trail Blazers reach the 2000 Western Conference Finals, which they lost to the Los Angeles Lakers in seven games.

Here's another question: When will Scottie win his next NBA championship? ★

Scottie's long arms and quickness make him a tough defender.

FAST FACTS

☆ Played on six NBA championship teams with the Chicago Bulls between 1991 and 1998
☆ Won gold medals with the 1992 and 1996 U.S. Olympic teams
☆ Named to NBA's All-Defensive first or second team every year from 1991 through 2000

JASON KIDD

Guard, Phoenix Suns
Born: March 23, 1973, in San Francisco, California
Height: 6' 4"
Weight: 212 pounds
Entered NBA: 1994

When it comes to giving, only Santa Claus does it better than Jason Kidd of the Phoenix Suns. Every day is Christmas when the 6' 4" point guard steps onto the court. Jason's presents come in the form of pinpoint passes to open teammates. No wonder he's such a popular member of the Suns!

"He knows how to play, and he seems to make everyone better," says former Sun guard Kevin Johnson.

That's what people used to say about Magic Johnson (no relation to Kevin). Magic won five NBA championships as a member of the Los Angeles Lakers. He was a terrific passer who would look to his left and pass to his right. It was something called a no-look pass, and Magic was great at it!

When he was growing up in Oakland, California, Jason idolized Magic. Jason was usually one of the first players selected for pickup games at the playground — not because he racked up the points. "Everybody wanted to score baskets," he says. "I would get picked a lot because they knew I wouldn't shoot."

These days, Jason shoots — and scores — for the Suns. He averaged 14.3 points per game during the 1999-2000 season. But he still specializes in assists. (An assist is awarded to the player who makes a pass that leads directly to a basket.) In 1998-99, Jason led the NBA in assists with an average of 10.8 per game. The following season, he averaged 10.1, also the best in the league.

"Jason Kidd is phenomenal," says Houston Rocket coach Rudy Tomjanovich. "The guy is such a winner, such a gamer, he's amazing. He's one of the best competitors I've ever seen."

That's some compliment to pass around! ★

The Kidd's alright! Jason is one of the NBA's top playmakers.

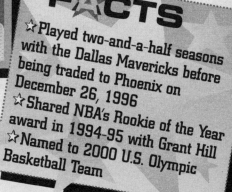

FAST FACTS

☆ Played two-and-a-half seasons with the Dallas Mavericks before being traded to Phoenix on December 26, 1996

☆ Shared NBA's Rookie of the Year award in 1994-95 with Grant Hill

☆ Named to 2000 U.S. Olympic Basketball Team

CHRIS WEBBER

Forward, Sacramento Kings
Born: March 1, 1973, in Detroit, Michigan
Height: 6' 10"
Weight: 245 pounds
Entered NBA: 1993

When forward Chris Webber of the Sacramento Kings first reached the NBA, in 1993, he wanted to buy something special for his father, Mayce [MAY-see]. So he bought him a brand new Cadillac!

The gift was a thoughtful one. Chris remembered how his dad had worked on a Cadillac assembly line in Detroit, Michigan. Mr. Webber put in long hours to support his wife, Doris, and their five children.

The Kings became a force after Chris joined them in 1998.

Mrs. Webber was a special-education teacher. She kept Chris focused on his studies. She made sure he attended Detroit Country Day, one of the top academic high schools in Michigan. Most of Chris's friends, including current NBA star Jalen Rose, went to inner city high schools in Detroit.

FAST FACTS

☆ Averaged at least 20 points per game each season from 1994-95 through 1999-2000
☆ Helped the University of Michigan reach the NCAA Championship game in each of his two seasons at the school
☆ Nickname is C. Webb

Chris missed his buddies, but the move paid off. He earned a diploma and won a basketball scholarship to the University of Michigan. Chris was even reunited with Jalen! The two were part of a fabulous recruiting class at Michigan known as the Fab Five.

Chris entered the NBA draft, in 1993, after spending two years in college. The Orlando Magic selected him first overall, but immediately traded him to the Golden State Warriors. Chris played one season with the Warriors and four with the Washington Wizards before being traded to Sacramento in 1998.

That move was a good one. Chris averaged 20 points and 13 rebounds per game in 1998-99. The following season, he averaged 24.5 points and 10.5 rebounds.

"He's the heart and soul of their team," says Kobe Bryant of the Los Angeles Lakers. ★

STEPHON MARBURY

Guard, New Jersey Nets
Born: February 20, 1977, in Brooklyn, New York
Height: 6' 2"
Weight: 180 pounds
Entered NBA: 1996

NBA careers are like roller coasters. There are highs, lows, and plenty of scary turns along the way. New Jersey Net guard Stephon Marbury knows all about roller coasters. He grew up in the Coney Island section of Brooklyn, New York. Coney Island has an amusement park with a world-famous thrill ride. Stephon and the Nets haven't given their fans a lot of thrills, but Stephon's career is definitely on the rise!

Stephon's scoring average went up in each of his first four NBA seasons. As a rookie, in 1996-97, he averaged 15.8 points per game for the Minnesota Timberwolves. During the 1999-2000 season, he averaged 22.2 points for New Jersey!

"You have to stay in front of Stephon," says Seattle Super-Sonic guard Gary Payton. "If he gets by you, he's trouble."

Stephon comes from a basketball family — a large one. He has four brothers and two sisters. All four of his brothers played basketball in college. When it was Stephon's turn, he chose Georgia Tech, in Atlanta. After just one season there, he jumped to the Timberwolves in 1996.

Minnesota featured two of the NBA's bright young stars in Stephon and Kevin Garnett. They were good friends and loved playing together, but Stephon was homesick. Midway through the 1998-99 season, he was traded to New Jersey. The deal made Stephon very happy because he got to move closer to his family. (The Nets' home court is only half an hour from New York City.)

Like the roller coaster in Coney Island, Stephon is making a slow climb to the top. And like that exciting ride, he will keep fans on the edge of their seats! ★

Stephon's biggest strength is his ability to handle the ball at top speed.

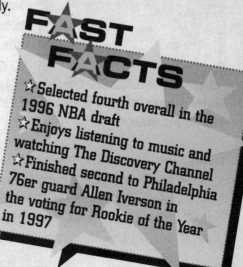

FAST FACTS

☆ Selected fourth overall in the 1996 NBA draft

☆ Enjoys listening to music and watching The Discovery Channel

☆ Finished second to Philadelphia 76er guard Allen Iverson in the voting for Rookie of the Year in 1997

JOHN STOCKTON

John's specialty is finding the open man.

Guard, Utah Jazz
Born: March 26, 1962, in Spokane, Washington
Height: 6' 1"
Weight: 175 pounds
Entered NBA: 1984

He's the NBA's all-time leader in assists and steals, but John Stockton can still get lost in a crowd. And that's a good thing. Unlike most players, the point guard of the Utah Jazz is uncomfortable in the spotlight. After games, his top priority is to get home to his wife, Nada, and their five children.

John's a throwback. There's not a lot of flash to his game, but few players have been more effective. A behind-the-back pass? Why bother when a simple bounce pass will do? John's not a dunker, but he's one of the best shooters in

NBA history. Try 51.8 percent from the field and 38.2 percent from behind the 3-point line! Want more? Check out his shorts. While most players have gone to the long, baggy look, John prefers to wear his at mid-thigh.

No duo in NBA history has combined for more baskets than the Jazz pair of John Stockton and Karl

FAST FACTS

☆ Set NBA's single-season assist record (1,164) in 1990-91
☆ Named one of the 50 greatest players in NBA history in 1996
☆ Missed only 22 games in his first 16 seasons
☆ Played college ball at Gonzaga University, in Spokane, Washington

Malone. John entered the league in 1984 (that's probably before you were born!). Karl followed a year later. They've spent their entire careers with Utah, and the team has never had a losing record during that time. Through 1999-2000, the Jazz had made the playoffs in each of John's 16 seasons. They reached the NBA Finals in 1997 and 1998, before losing to Michael Jordan's Chicago Bulls.

John's the playmaker while Karl is a bruising power forward. Friends off the court, they have a remarkable chemistry on it. "I always expect the perfect pass from John," says Karl. "And I always get it."

Few players have been more durable than John. He once played 609 games in a row! He led the NBA in assists nine straight years, from 1987-88 to 1995-96.

Impressive numbers for sure. But don't expect John to hang around and talk about them. He'll take a *pass*!   ★

KARL MALONE

Forward, Utah Jazz
Born: July 24, 1963, in
Summerfield, Louisiana
Height: 6' 9"
Weight: 256 pounds
Entered NBA: 1985

Karl Malone of the Utah Jazz has done impressive things on the basketball court. The power forward became the third-leading scorer in NBA history in 2000. Through 1999-2000, he had won two MVP awards and had been named First Team All-NBA for 11 consecutive seasons. Those are Hall-of-Fame credentials.

He delivers! Karl remains one of the NBA's best-conditioned athletes.

But here's the most impressive feat of all: In 15 NBA seasons, Karl had missed just six games. That's what you call durability! It's amazing that Karl has never had a serious injury, especially because he plays a position that is very demanding physically. Power forwards have to battle for rebounds under the boards. They have to muscle their way to the hoop and score against other big, strong play- ers. It's not a job for the weak or timid.

FAST FACTS

☆In 1996, named one of the 50 greatest players in NBA history
☆Named MVP of the NBA All-Star Game in 1989 and 1993
☆In 1998, became the only player in NBA history to score at least 2,000 points in 11 consecutive seasons

How has Karl remained in the lineup? He takes care of his 6' 9", 256-pound body. He may be the best-conditioned player in the NBA. He runs, lifts weights, and uses a step-climbing machine known as the StairMaster.

"Luck, conditioning, and playing hard is what keeps me healthy," Karl says. "When you let down your intensity, you're more likely to get hurt."

No one plays with more passion than Karl. He averaged 25.5 points per game in 1999-2000 — at the age of 36! That was fifth best in the league. On January 29, 2000, in a game against the Minnesota Timberwolves, he became just the third player in league history to reach the 30,000-point mark. He finished the 1999-2000 season with 31,041 career points. Only legendary Hall of Famers Kareem Abdul-Jabbar (38,387) and Wilt Chamberlain (31,419) have scored more in a career!

> **"I'm the meanest person in the world on the court . . . But when the game ends, I'll be the first guy to shake your hand."**
> **— Karl Malone, Utah Jazz forward**

Karl is someone who delivers. That's why a Louisiana sportswriter nicknamed him "The Mailman" when Karl played for Louisiana Tech University. He was drafted by the Jazz in 1985 and has never played on a losing team in Utah. A big reason for that is the way he approaches the game. Although he is friendly off the court, Karl becomes a different person once he hits the hardwood.

"I don't play this game so that people will like me," he says. "I'm the meanest person in the world on the court. I'll step on you. But when the game ends, I'll be the first guy to shake your hand."

Lots of folks were shaking Karl's hand in 1997. That's when he won his first MVP award, beating out Michael Jordan. Karl also won it in 1999, the year after Michael retired. The honors are nice, but Karl wants to win an NBA championship before finishing his career. The Jazz have come close, but lost to the Chicago Bulls in the 1997 and 1998 NBA Finals.

Children are important to Karl. In 1997, he established a foundation to help kids in need. The foundation raises money for children suffering from illness or other problems. Karl has been called the greatest power forward in NBA history. But he's also a powerful guy when it comes to helping others! ★

Stars of the Future

So far, you've been reading about the best basketball players of today. But what about the stars of tomorrow? Who might be on the cover of *Basketball All-Stars* five years from now? The great thing about the NBA is that new and exciting players enter the league every season. That was certainly the case in 1999-2000. Four rookies established themselves as players to watch. We think they have the talent, skill, and attitude to become superstars.

Steve Francis of the Houston Rockets and Elton Brand of the Chicago Bulls shared the NBA's Rookie of the Year award for the 1999-2000 season. Steve's a flashy guard from the University of Maryland. He averaged 18 points per game in his rookie year. Elton, a rugged power forward from Duke University, averaged more than 20 points and 10 rebounds a game. Those are great numbers for a veteran, let alone a first-year player! Forwards Lamar Odom of the Los Angeles Clippers and Wally Szczerbiak of the Minnesota Timberwolves also enjoyed solid rookie seasons.

So keep reading and learn more about the Stars of the Future! ★

STEVE FRANCIS

Guard, Houston Rockets
Born: February 21, 1977, in Silver Spring, Maryland
Height: 6' 3"
Weight: 193 pounds
Entered NBA: 1999

Steve Francis started 77 games as a rookie point guard for the Houston Rockets during the 1999-2000 season. That's 76 more than he started during his entire high school career!

That's amazing, but it's true. Things did not come easily for Steve at Montgomery Blair High School, in Silver Spring, Maryland. In 10th grade, he was just 5' 3" tall. He made the team, but he was usually a third-string guard. That turned out to be his only season of high school basketball.

Steve grew almost a foot by his senior year, but other problems kept him off the court. He did poorly in school, partly because his mother, Brenda Wilson, got very sick with cancer. She died at age 39, in March of his senior year. Steve was so upset he didn't graduate from high school.

It would have been easy for Steve to give up. He didn't, though. He was becoming too good a basketball player.

Steve played daily pickup games in the gym of a local firehouse. He earned his high school equivalency diploma.

That was Steve's ticket to college. After attending two different schools, he landed at the University of Maryland in 1998. Steve led the Terrapins to a school-record 28 wins during the 1998-99 season.

Steve entered the 1999 NBA draft and was selected second overall by the Vancouver Grizzlies. Two months later, he was traded to Houston.

During the 1999-2000 season, Steve led NBA rookies in assists (6.6 per game) while finishing second in scoring (18 points per game). He shared the league's Rookie of the Year award with Elton Brand of the Chicago Bulls.

Steve was an NBA sensation. You might say he *rocketed* to success! ★

Steve overcame plenty of adversity before reaching the NBA.

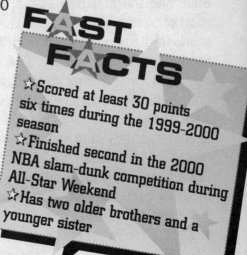

FAST FACTS

☆ Scored at least 30 points six times during the 1999-2000 season

☆ Finished second in the 2000 NBA slam-dunk competition during All-Star Weekend

☆ Has two older brothers and a younger sister

ELTON BRAND

Forward, Chicago Bulls
Born: March 11, 1979, in Peekskill, New York
Height: 6' 8"
Weight: 260 pounds
Entered NBA: 1999

Jerry Krause, the vice president of basketball operations for the Chicago Bulls, had a tough decision to make. The Bulls had the first pick in the 1999 NBA draft and several good players were available. One of them was Elton Brand, a bruising power forward from Duke University. There was Steve Francis, a flashy guard from the University of Maryland, and Lamar Odom, a big-time scorer from the University of Rhode Island. Whom would the Bulls choose?

Mr. Krause was most impressed with Elton. He liked Elton's maturity and willingness to work hard. That was important because the Bulls were rebuilding. Michael Jordan had retired. Scottie Pippen and head coach Phil Jackson had also left the team. Chicago had gone from being the NBA's best team to one of its worst. Mr. Krause thought Elton was a player the Bulls could build around.

That's why he made him the number 1 pick.

It was a great choice! Elton led all rookies in points (20.1), rebounds (10), minutes played (37), and blocked shots (1.63) per game. His scoring average improved every month of the season, from 16.2, in November, to 24.3, in April. Elton was named MVP of the Rookie All-Star Game, and shared the league's Rookie of the Year award with Steve Francis of the Houston Rockets.

Future star? Absolutely! Elton is a terrific scorer and rebounder.

"[Elton] competes, he cares about defense, and he just really plays hard," says Bull coach Tim Floyd.

Elton is 6' 8" — short for a power forward — but he has huge hands, long arms, and a muscular build.

That's good because the future of the Bulls rests on his broad shoulders. ★

FAST FACTS

☆ Became first player from Duke University to be chosen first overall in the NBA draft

☆ Won several college Player of the Year awards as a sophomore, in 1998-99

☆ Missed 15 games as a freshman at Duke after breaking his left foot

LAMAR ODOM

Forward, Los Angeles Clippers
Born: **November 6, 1979,** in **Jamaica, New York**
Height: **6' 10"**
Weight: **220 pounds**
Entered NBA: **1999**

When an NBA player is drafted, one of the first things he usually buys is a flashy new car. Forward Lamar Odom of the Los Angeles Clippers didn't bother. Why? Because he didn't know how to drive!

Lamar grew up in New York City, where he rode subway trains to get around. His family didn't own a car. During his rookie season, with the Clippers, Lamar got rides from teammates or hired a driver to take him around Los Angeles.

Lamar scored 30 points in his NBA debut on November 2, 1999.

The only driving Lamar did was on the basketball court — and it was full speed ahead!

Lamar left his "tire tracks" on opponents' backs while averaging 16.6 points per game in 1999-2000. That was the third-best scoring average among NBA rookies. Only Elton Brand of the Chicago Bulls (20.1) and Steve Francis of the Houston Rockets (18.0) scored more. Lamar also averaged 7.8 rebounds and led his team with 4.2 assists per game.

"He's a very likeable person," said Elgin Baylor, the Clippers' vice president of basketball operations. "What I see him doing is making other players better because of his ability to pass the basketball and create scoring chances for other people."

Lamar caused quite a stir at the University of Rhode Island. He played there for only one season, but what a season it was! In 1998-99, Lamar averaged 17 points, 9.4 rebounds, and 3.8 assists per game. In the 1999 Atlantic 10 Conference championship game, Lamar hit a 3-pointer at the buzzer to give the Rams a 62–59 win over Temple University. The Clippers were so impressed that they chose him fourth overall in the 1999 NBA draft.

At 6' 10", Lamar can pass, shoot, and run the floor like a 6' guard. Car or no car, Lamar is going places! ★

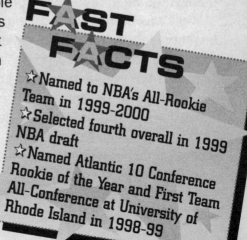

FAST FACTS

☆ Named to NBA's All-Rookie Team in 1999-2000

☆ Selected fourth overall in 1999 NBA draft

☆ Named Atlantic 10 Conference Rookie of the Year and First Team All-Conference at University of Rhode Island in 1998-99

WALLY SZCZERBIAK

Forward, Minnesota Timberwolves
Born: March 5, 1977, in Madrid, Spain
Height: 6' 8"
Weight: 248 pounds
Entered NBA: 1999

The first thing you need to know about Wally is how to pronounce his last name: *SIR-bee-ak*. It's a tongue-twister, and that's appropriate, because Wally's great shooting often turns defenders inside out.

Wally was born in Madrid, Spain. His dad, Walt, played pro basketball there for a team called Real [*ray-AL*] Madrid. Mr. Szczerbiak loved hoops and passed that love on to his son.

Wally's family later moved to Long Island, New York. Wally worked hard to become a star at Cold Spring Harbor High School. As a senior, he averaged 36.6 points per game! That was impressive, but many top colleges chose not to recruit him. They wondered if the league Wally played in was tough enough.

So Wally attended little Miami University, in Oxford, Ohio, and kept working to prove himself. By his junior season, many people were calling him the best college player in the country. Wally averaged 24.4 points per game as a junior and 24.2 as a senior. He shot better than 52 percent from the field both seasons.

The Minnesota Timberwolves selected Wally with the sixth overall pick in the 1999 NBA draft. "I had no plans of sitting on the bench," he said, reflecting on his rookie season. Not to worry! Wally started 53 of the 73 games he played in 1999-2000. He made 51.1 percent of his field-goal attempts (second-best among NBA rookies) and 35.9 percent of his 3-pointers (fourth-best). With an average of 11.6 points per game (fifth among rookies), Wally was a shoo-in for the NBA's All-Rookie Team.

The only thing tougher than stopping Wally may be pronouncing his last name. Maybe you should just call him future All-Star! ★

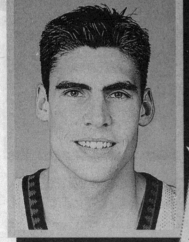

Wally was the best shooter available in the 1999 NBA draft.

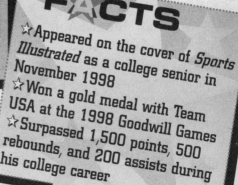

FAST FACTS

☆ Appeared on the cover of *Sports Illustrated* as a college senior in November 1998

☆ Won a gold medal with Team USA at the 1998 Goodwill Games

☆ Surpassed 1,500 points, 500 rebounds, and 200 assists during his college career

CHARLES BARKLEY

**Forward,
Philadelphia 76ers,
Phoenix Suns, and
Houston Rockets
Born:** February 20, 1963,
**in Leeds, Alabama
Height:** 6' 6"
Weight: 252 pounds
Entered NBA: 1984
Retired: 2000

When Charles Barkley retired from the NBA after the 1999-2000 season, it was a loss for fans, teammates, opponents, and NBA

Charles scored 23,757 points and grabbed 12,546 rebounds in his NBA career.

reporters. Especially reporters. Year after year, basketball writers selected Charles for the league's All-Interview Team.

Sir Charles, as he was nicknamed, is a funny guy. Even after he stopped playing pro hoops, he continued to attract

Tribute

some of the biggest crowds on the Celebrity Golf Tour. It wasn't because he played like Tiger Woods. He didn't. Fans came to hear his jokes and rants. They often came away with tears streaming down their faces because Charles made them laugh so hard!

Charles had as many opinions as jokes. He wasn't shy about sharing them, either, even if they were unpopular opinions. "I say the things that I feel are right," Charles says. "I don't always say the things people want to hear."

On the basketball court, Charles made his presence known with his awesome play. In 16 seasons with the Philadelphia 76ers, Phoenix Suns, and Houston Rockets, he played on nine All-Star teams and won the league's MVP award once, in 1992-93. All told, he played 1,073 regular-season games and averaged 22.1 points, 11.7 rebounds, and 3.9 assists per contest. In 1996, he was voted one of the 50 greatest players in NBA history!

Few players were more ferocious on the boards than Charles. He used his brick-solid body to overpower smaller opponents, and he used his smarts to score on the bigger ones. He could run the floor and score off a fast break. Charles was also a good pressure player who demanded the ball in clutch situations. More often than not, he delivered the big basket.

"I have so many great memories," Charles says. "I thank God I have this huge brain that can keep all these memories stored."

And, of course, he delivered the laughs, too.　　★

WANT TO HAVE MORE FUN

WITH SPORTS ILLUSTRATED FOR KIDS?

GET A FREE TRIAL ISSUE of SPORTS ILLUSTRATED FOR KIDS magazine. Each monthly issue is jam-packed with awesome athletes, super-sized photos, cool sports facts, comics, games, and jokes!

Ask your mom or dad to call and order your free trial issue today! The phone number is 1-800-732-5080.

PLUG IN TO www.sikids.com. That's the S.I. FOR KIDS website on the Internet. You'll find great games, free fantasy leagues, sports news, trivia quizzes, and more.

CHECK OUT S.I. FOR KIDS Weekly in the comic section of many newspapers. It has lots of cool photos, stories, and puzzles from the Number 1 sports magazine for kids!

LOOK FOR more S.I. FOR KIDS books. They make reading **fun!**